drawnandquarterly.com

ISBN 978-1-77046-402-5

First edition: October 2020 | Printed in China | 10 9 8 7 6 5 4 3 2 1

Cataloguing data available from Library and Archives Canada

Published in the USA by Drawn & Quarterly, a client publisher of Farrar, Straus and Giroux
Published in Canada by Drawn & Quarterly, a client publisher of Raincoast Books
Published in the United Kingdom by Drawn & Quarterly, a client publisher of Publishers Group UK

Drawn & Quarterly acknowledges the support of the Government of Canada and the Canada Council for the Arts for our publishing program, and the National Translation Program for Book Publishing, an initiative of the Roadmap for Canada's Official Languages 2013-2019: Education, Immigration, Communities, for our translation activities.

Drawn & Quarterly reconnaît l'aide financière du gouvernement du Québec par l'entremise de la Société de développement des entreprises culturelles (SODEC) pour nos activités d'édition. Gouvernement du Québec—Programme de crédit d'impôt pour l'édition de livres—Gestion SODEC.

Cet ouvrage a bénéficié du soutien des Programmes d'aide à la publication de l'Institut français.

THE LEAGUE OF SUPER FEMINISTS

MIRION MALLE

TRANSLATED BY ALESHIA JENSEN

DRAWN & QUARTERLY

✦ Representation ✦

Movies and TV shows are pretty much the best ever.

I watch about ten thousand a day.

When my eyes get too sore, I take reading breaks.

IT'S SO COOL TO HAVE SO MANY STORIES TO CHOOSE FROM AND TO IMAGINE YOU'RE A...

Singer

Knight

Fighter

etc.!

?

Um, I can't think of many stories where girls are Knights.

Argh. Unfortunately, you're right. That's exactly the problem!

There are LOTS of stories out there, but they're full of STEREOTYPES.*

*A STEREOTYPE is a premade idea that doesn't actually correspond to real life, but is something we hear so often that it ends up seeming real.

FOR EXAMPLE

"Girls are fragile and boys are strong."

SEXIST STEREOTYPE ON THE LOOSE!!!!!!

→ A stereotype is sexist when it's based on someone's gender.

grrrr

I'm a girl, so I'm wild for love.

BASICALLY, IT'S ALWAYS THE SAME CHARACTERS IN GENDER-BASED ROLES:

Knight   princess   tough guy   singer   top model   intellectual

And if we dig a little deeper, we find even MORE problems, EVERYWHERE we look!

Everyone is white

There are rarely any girls

The guys are (pretty much) ALWAYS the HERO

...and they get made fun of if they like "girl" things

Everyone is thin

So, the subtext is that being a girl is embarrassing...great!

That's so silly!

But at the same time: is it really that big of a deal?

Well...for starters, seeing the same stories over and over gets kinda boring!

L I K E

A Princess Gets Married

The Princess Gets Married the movie

Coming soon: the new TV show A Princess Wedding

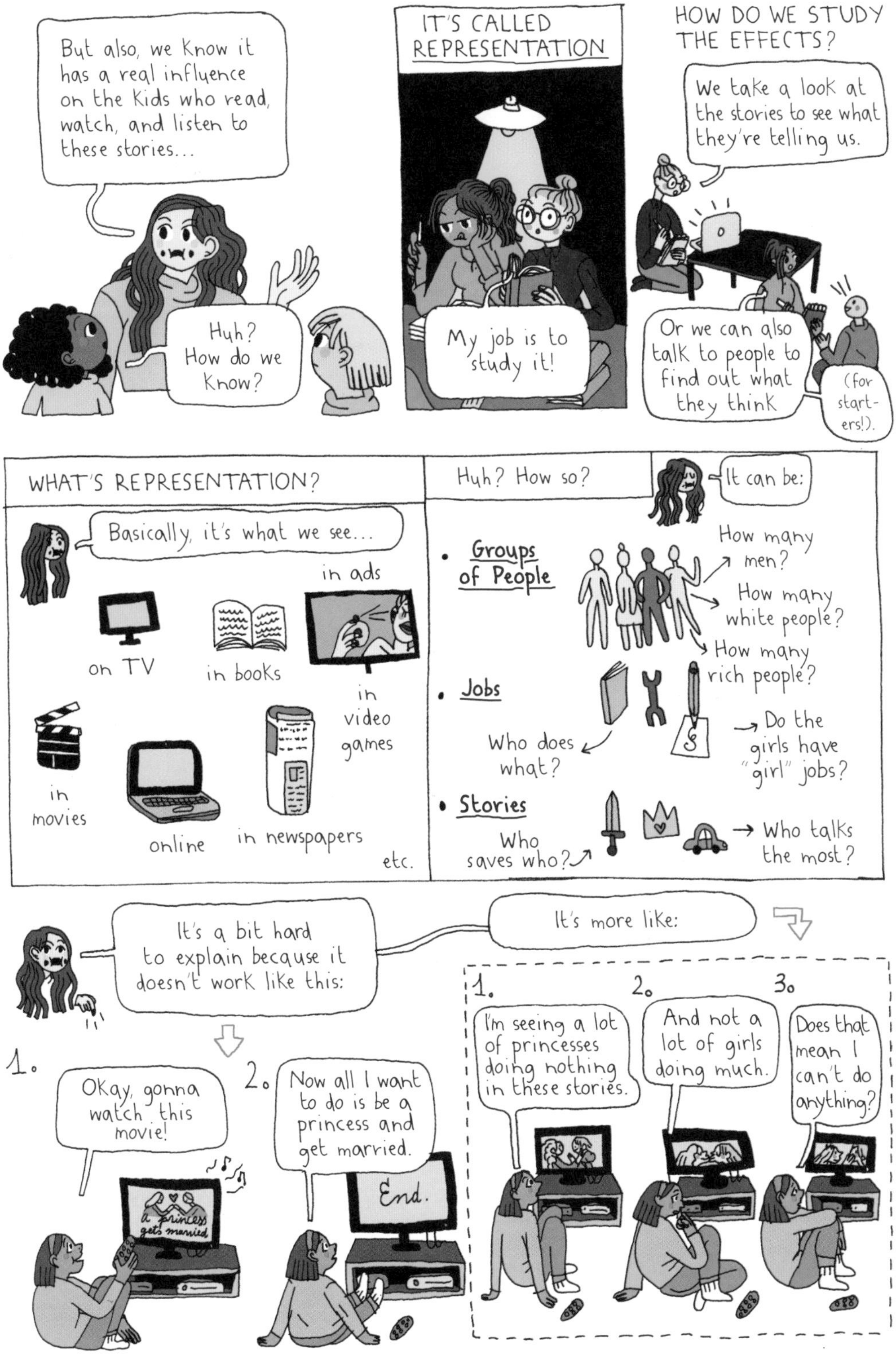
But also, we know it has a real influence on the kids who read, watch, and listen to these stories...
Huh? How do we know?
IT'S CALLED REPRESENTATION
My job is to study it!
HOW DO WE STUDY THE EFFECTS?
We take a look at the stories to see what they're telling us.
Or we can also talk to people to find out what they think
(for starters!).
WHAT'S REPRESENTATION?
Basically, it's what we see...
on TV
in books
in ads
in video games
in movies
online
in newspapers
etc.
Huh? How so?
It can be:
Groups of People
How many men?
How many white people?
How many rich people?
Jobs
Who does what?
Do the girls have "girl" jobs?
Stories
Who saves who?
Who talks the most?
It's a bit hard to explain because it doesn't work like this:
1.
Okay, gonna watch this movie!
a princess gets married
2.
Now all I want to do is be a princess and get married.
End.
It's more like:
1.
I'm seeing a lot of princesses doing nothing in these stories.
2.
And not a lot of girls doing much.
3.
Does that mean I can't do anything?

THE GEENA DAVIS INSTITUTE IN THE UNITED STATES LOOKS SPECIFICALLY AT REPRESENTATION.

Especially of girls!

(Geena Davis is an actor and has played tons of really awesome strong female characters.)

The institute shows how little girls develop big complexes about how they look...

I want to be pretty!!

I should lose weight!

...and about what they can do!

I'm bad at sports.

Am I terrible at science?

I can't manage by myself...

(FOR EXAMPLE...)

HERE ARE A BUNCH OF REASONS WHY THIS MIGHT HAPPEN:

→ The girl characters are often portrayed as sexy (even kids!!)

→ They're always SUPER SKINNY

→ They're often either slightly or not at all important

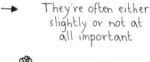

gets saved

saves everyone

etc.

THE RESULT:

BY AGE 8, GIRLS START FEELING LESS CONFIDENT IN THEMSELVES...

I can't do this...

yuck

(AND BY AGE 10, MANY GIRLS THINK THEIR STOMACHS LOOK FAT...)

And it only gets worse... For example, between ages 18 and 25, 1 OUT OF 2 GIRLS would rather be run over by a truck than be fat...

Can you believe that???

But umm...

Does that mean we can't watch princess movies anymore?

'Cause uhh...I like watching them sometimes...and romance movies too... but only sometimes...

No no, it'd be kinda sad if we couldn't watch them at all!

Luckily we can watch whatever we want!

WE JUST NEED TO **UNDERSTAND** WHAT WE'RE SEEING AND **REALLY THINK ABOUT IT!**

And not be afraid of <u>criticizing it</u>!!!

AND THAT REQUIRES <u>TOOLS</u>!

(Not these kinds)

What I mean is <u>intellectual</u> tools!

Woohoo!

LIKE FOR EXAMPLE

The SUPER POWER of reading between the lines!!

And lots of other ones we'll learn about together in this B O O K !

THE BECHDEL TEST

The Bechdel test is a tool that lets us take a look at the role of women in the media we consume!

THE NAME COMES FROM ALISON BECHDEL, an American cartoonist!

The test is named after me but it's my friend Liz Wallace who came up with the idea!

• HOW DOES IT WORK? •

1. We take a piece of media:

movie

TV show

book

etc.

2. Are there at least two female characters with a name?

That girl

What's-her-name

3. Are there at least two female characters who talk to each other?

blah

blah blah

4. Do they talk about something besides a guy?

blah

It seems super simple, but in reality, not that many films pass the test!

Try it with your favorite movies!

→ The website bechdeltest.com shows that only 57.6% of 8076 movies they've analyzed pass the test!*

(That's not very many!)

IT DOESN'T MEAN THAT A MOVIE THAT DOESN'T PASS THE TEST IS SEXIST (or the opposite)

It might be that there's only one character in the movie, for example.

Or that... um...it's a silent movie.

BUT IT STILL SHOWS THAT THERE'S A REAL LACK OF WOMEN IN THE STORIES BEING TOLD!

* These statistics were retrieved in January 2019

Friendship

For the most part, friendship is a beautiful thing!

YOU GET TO DO LOTS OF COOL THINGS!

blahblah

hahahaha

- SPEND 1000 YEARS ON THE PHONE

- MAKE SUPER HILARIOUS JOKES

- RIDE AROUND SUPER FAST

(for example...)

IN REAL LIFE, FRIENDSHIP CAN LOOK HOWEVER WE WANT IT TO!

friends *friends* *friends*

But if we take a close look at the kinds of stories out there, friendship is generally reserved for boys...hmm...

EXAMPLES

GRR

Girls are often shown as rivals...

Or they're just there to be in love with boys...

Sometimes, they're even rivals fighting over a BOY'S AFFECTION!!!

There are obviously exceptions, but usually we see only one (that's right: ONE) girl in a group of guy friends.

Because there are lots of boys, they all have different personalities: jokester, geek, tough guy, athlete...But since there's only one girl, she's just "THE GIRL": her gender* is her only personality trait.

*"gender" is what we call the different social roles assigned to girls and boys.

 Like Smurfette, for instance.

And sometimes boys fall in love with us. That's all we're here for, hehe!

Uhh

I think we can all agree that's NOT COOL!!

INCREDIBLE

Girls and boys can be FRIENDS with each other !!!!!

Double-INCREDIBLE

GIRLS ARE FULLY FLEDGED HUMAN BEINGS!

Who'd a thought...?

SUMMING UP A FEMALE CHARACTER AS JUST "THE GIRL" = OBVIOUSLY NOT SUPER GREAT. BECAUSE IT MEANS THAT GIRLS WATCHING THE TV SHOW OR MOVIE ARE ASKED TO IDENTIFY WITH THE DIFFERENT PERSONALITIES OF THE BOYS, BUT IT'S ASSUMED THAT THE BOYS WATCHING WOULD NEVER IDENTIFY WITH A GIRL.

So this is Ben. He likes pizza and his favorite subject is math.

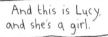

And this is Lucy, and she's a girl.

It seems ridiculous to have to say this, but girls have all sorts of different personalities, interests, strengths and weaknesses, just like boys do!!! And it seems like this should be OBVIOUS!

For instance, I like... martial arts, Knights, make-up, the ocean, comedy, animals, food, drag queens, comic books, running, movies, poetry, roundhouse Kicks, Jean-Claude Van Damme, dinosaurs, hiking, summer-time, music, flowers, rocks, dumpling

Okay, we get the point!

So, that means we're fully fledged human beings, just as capable of interacting with other human beings. And therefore, capable of having friends, just like guys are!

Yeah!!!

STORIES ABOUT FRIENDSHIP BETWEEN GIRLS OFTEN GO A BIT LIKE THIS:

  VS

nice girls   mean girls

ARG! So already we've got girls being pitted against each other all the time! IT'S SO FRUSTRATING!!

Not only is it rare to see friendship between girls represented...

Stories where there might be girls who are friends:

stories for little girls

stories for teen girls

stories for women

Stories where there are boys who're friends:

100% of stories, even the ones "for girls"

...but in the rare cases we do see girls who are friends, they're fighting with each other....

AND WHAT'S MORE, THE "MEAN" GIRLS ARE OFTEN CONSIDERED MEAN FOR SEXIST REASONS!

And this gives girls the idea that they should actually be competing with each other. When really, they should be <u>supporting each other</u>!

Because they wear make-up, for instance...

or because they date lots of boys...

(When really, these things are not a big deal.)

 But why? There are definitely mean girls out there too...

And I don't really want to be friends with them!

   Yes, for sure they exist! But it's important to stop and think about why exactly we think a girl is "mean."

Does she bully you?

Don't like her look?

She likes the same boy as you or your friend?

Insult you?

She's a jock?

Hit you?

She doesn't like the same things as you?

→ PROBABLY NOT SUPER NICE.

→ SHE'S PROBABLY A COOL PERSON!! Even though you're different or you aren't friends, that doesn't mean she's your enemy!

IT'S **VERY** IMPORTANT FOR US TO STICK TOGETHER

It's already really hard to be a girl today, because we live in a SEXIST society.

A sexist society is a society based on sexist ideas...

wah

Women love looking after babies

Women are naturally good at housework

What women think and say is less important than what men think and say

...that are used to justify a bunch of really serious things like:

Paying women less

People feeling like they have the right to control and comment on women's bodies

Violence

SO WE NEED TO BE THERE FOR EACH OTHER.

And that means considering ALL women so that no one is excluded, including people who look different than you!

Have you ever heard the phrase "divide and conquer"?

IT MEANS THAT IT'S EASIER TO OPPRESS AND EXPLOIT PEOPLE WHEN THEY'RE ALONE AND ANGRY AT EACH OTHER THAN WHEN THEY JOIN FORCES AND FIGHT BACK AS A GROUP.

I'm not saying we need to love every single girl out there as an individual. But it's important to support each other so we can resist these oppressive ideas!

Stop violence against women! We want equal pay! And we don't want to do all the housework! We want real equality!

YEAH! High five!

Um...can I be friends with you too?...

Okay, but you better not act sexist!!!!

gulp

Promise!!

♥ `Romance` ♥

Ah, loooooove!

We could go on for hours...all those thousands of songs, books, movies, poems, and what-have-yous about love!

Yeah but I'm so sick of seeing princesses getting saved by princes. And presto! They're in love! Hmph!

Hahahaha, yeah, true. Representation of love is often... uh...how shall I put it?

Total garbage.

OVER HERE YOU HAVE THE GIRL CHARACTERS WHO ONLY THINK ABOUT LOVE...

AND OVER HERE THE GUY CHARACTERS WHO HAVE A THOUSAND OTHER INTERESTS...

Don't you think it's a bit strange that we're always being told how much girls just adoooooore love? How it's the most important thing?

Yeah! It's almost like they're trying to convince us of something...

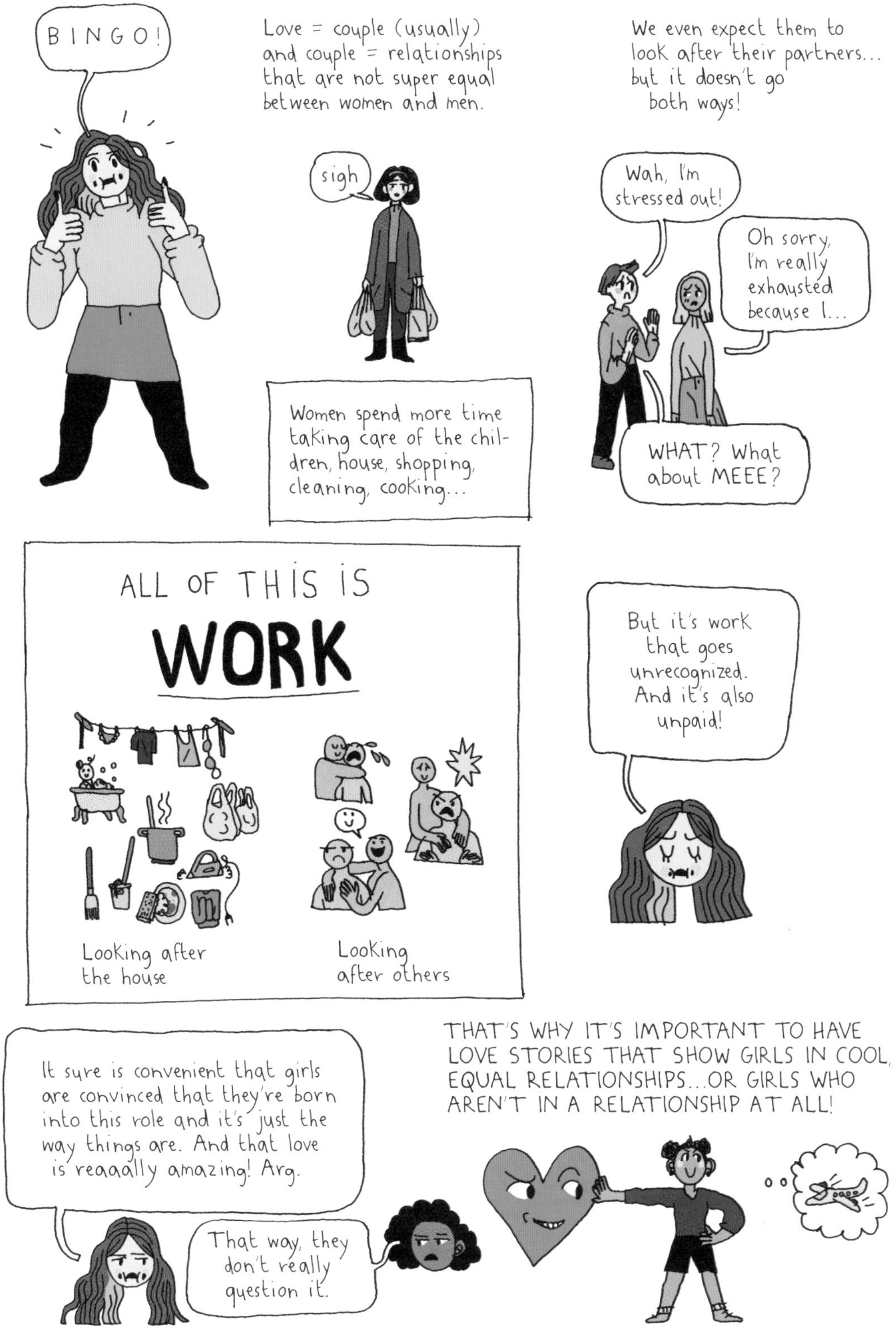
BINGO!
Love = couple (usually) and couple = relationships that are not super equal between women and men.
sigh
Women spend more time taking care of the children, house, shopping, cleaning, cooking...
We even expect them to look after their partners... but it doesn't go both ways!
Wah, I'm stressed out!
Oh sorry, I'm really exhausted because I...
WHAT? What about MEEE?
ALL OF THIS IS
WORK
Looking after the house
Looking after others
But it's work that goes unrecognized. And it's also unpaid!
It sure is convenient that girls are convinced that they're born into this role and it's just the way things are. And that love is reaaally amazing! Arg.
That way, they don't really question it.
THAT'S WHY IT'S IMPORTANT TO HAVE LOVE STORIES THAT SHOW GIRLS IN COOL, EQUAL RELATIONSHIPS...OR GIRLS WHO AREN'T IN A RELATIONSHIP AT ALL!

Also there's the fact that...
um...sometimes I have crushes
on other boys...and uhh...I
never see that on TV...

That's so
true and it's
a real problem!!

IT'S RARE TO SEE CHARACTERS
WHO LIKE SOMEONE OF THE
SAME GENDER EVEN IN MEDIA
FOR ADULTS AND TEENS.

BUT IN MEDIA FOR
KIDS, IT'S PRETTY
MUCH NEVER!

Why?

A lot of people have the dumb idea
that it isn't normal to like a girl when
you're a girl, or a boy when you're a
boy. They even think that it's bad.
This is what we call being homophobic.

Because of these people, there's this
weird idea that being queer,* or lik-
ing someone of the same gender as you,
is something sad, or even dangerous.
Basically, people think the whole thing
is too "complicated" for children!

HATE ⟶

But almost everyone
seems fine designat-
ing male-female
couples pretty much
from birth....

*Queer is an inclusive term sometimes used to describe people
who do not conform to sexual or gender "norms."

While in reality, it's awesome, it's perfectly normal, it's life!

What's sad about loving someone? It's a pretty great thing, no?

But my broken heart...sniff.

Aw, yes, that can happen too. And it's okay!

IN REAL LIFE, PEOPLE OF ALL GENDERS LIKE EACH OTHER.

And, spoiler alert: pretending they don't exist isn't going to make them heterosexual.*

IT'LL JUST MAKE THEM FEEL SAD OR CONFUSED, AND LIKE IT'S NOT NORMAL.

*Someone who's attracted to people of the opposite gender. Another word for this is "straight."

THE MOST IMPORTANT THING ABOUT LOVE IS TO ALWAYS TREAT THE OTHER PERSON WITH **RESPECT** AND MAKE SURE THEY ARE COMFORTABLE AND FINE WITH EVERYTHING.

Be Kind to your fellow human beings!

Please!

Is it okay if I hold your hand?

Yeah!!!

23

CONSENT

Consent is making sure that when people do something together, EVERYONE wants to do it.

IT SHOULD APPLY TO EVERYTHING. WE CAN'T FORCE SOMEONE TO

EAT DRINK PLAY, etc.

BUT WE MOST OFTEN USE IT WHEN TALKING ABOUT...

THINGS WE DO WITH PEOPLE WE'RE IN LOVE WITH!

WE CAN'T FORCE SOMEONE TO BE IN LOVE WITH US OR TO DO THE TYPE OF THINGS WE DO WHEN WE'RE IN LOVE.

So we always need to make sure everyone is having a good time!

Can I Kiss you?

Yes!!

↳ Okay!!

No!

↳ Not okay!!

Um...I'm not sure...

↳ Not okay!!

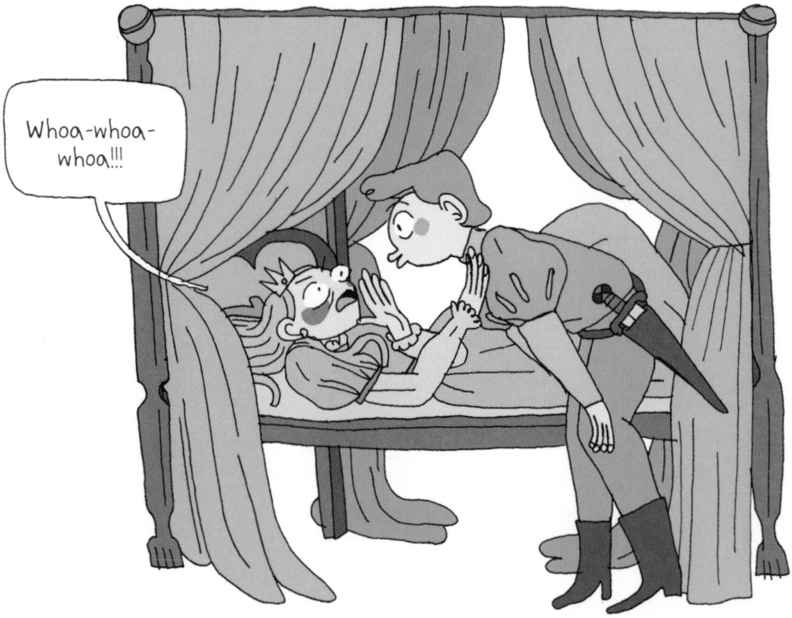
Whoa-whoa-whoa!!!

Beauty

When it comes to female characters, we all have one thing in common: our physical appearances always seem to be very important.

Such as:

ahem

"Her long blond hair fell down the back of her short, green dress."

And guess what? It's the same when you read about women in real life too!

"Wearing a blouse that brings out her bright eyes..."

"The official's long hair framed her smiling face."

"She's the karate champion, but above all, she's a chic young lady..."

And obviously it's different for men. We talk about their personality, work, actions...

How come?

To force us to think about our appearance!

Yep...Society values women based on how they look, unfortunately.

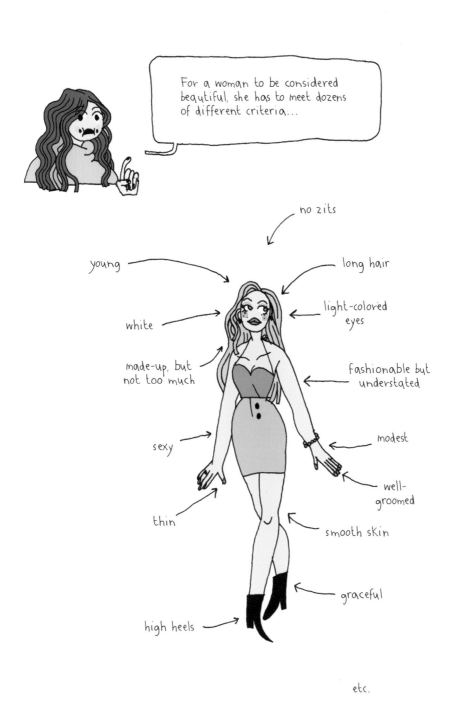

PUTTING SO MUCH EMPHASIS ON HOW WOMEN
LOOK HAS SERIOUS CONSEQUENCES!

CONSEQUENCE 1: EVERYONE FEELS THEY HAVE THE RIGHT TO JUDGE AND COMMENT ON WOMEN'S BODIES AND CLOTHING!

Since women's importance is reduced to their appearance, people seem to think they can have their say.

But it's for their own good!!

Nobody asked for your opinion!!

Women's bodies belong to them alone.

UNWANTED COMMENTS ON APPEARANCE ARE NOT OKAY!

Put on a little weight, hey?

BUT SOME MEN EVEN FEEL ENTITLED TO HARASS COMPLETE STRANGERS...

Give us a smile, sweetheart!

SUPERMAR

It would never cross anyone's mind to say that to a guy, and yet we let girls think it's okay to be talked to this way—that it's normal!!

WHETHER THEY'RE CONSIDERED TOO SEXY...

Skank!

OR NOT SEXY ENOUGH...

Try a bit harder, will ya?

➡️ GIRLS ARE CRITICIZED NO MATTER WHAT AND CAN NEVER GET A MINUTE'S PEACE!

CONSEQUENCE 2: ONLY PRETTY GIRLS ARE REPRESENTED

→ Even the "ugly" girls in movies are way too conventionally attractive!!!

OPTION 1
Top model with glasses

OPTION 2
Top model with bad clothes

OPTION 3
Top model with glasses and bad clothes

BUT GUYS ARE SHOWN IN ALL SHAPES, SIZES, AND STYLES...

STOCKY, BUFF, SHORT, AVERAGE, SKINNY...
AND NOT ALWAYS SUPER GOOD LOOKING!

BUT THE GIRLS ALL LOOK LIKE THEY'VE POPPED OUT OF THE SAME MOLD.

And if a girl doesn't fit into this standard mold, it's pointed out.

For example, bigger girls are often included as a joke, and rarely considered pretty...

Which is why a lot of girls would rather be run over by a truck than gain weight*...

HA HA

*See chapter 1

CONSEQUENCE 3:
WHITE GIRLS ARE SHOWN AS THE MOST ATTRACTIVE

RACISM IS EVERYWHERE IN THE BEAUTY INDUSTRY AND IN THE IMAGES THEY SHOW US, INCLUDING:

straight hair (usually blond)

light-colored eyes

pale skin and rosy cheeks

→ WHITE PEOPLE'S CHARACTERISTICS

THERE'S ALREADY VERY FEW PEOPLE OF COLOR REPRESENTED....

AND THEN THE WOMEN OF COLOR SHOWN AS PRETTY ARE OFTEN RACIST STEREOTYPES:

"the Black guy"

"the girl"

ten thousand white dudes

meek geisha

hip hop gangsta sexy and wild

belly dancer

EITHER THAT, OR THEY'RE TOLD TO LOOK AS WHITE AS POSSIBLE...

BECAUSE OTHERWISE, SOCIETY REJECTS THEM.

whether it's hair relaxers

skin lightening products

or even eyelid surgery

Uh-uh, no afros at school.

Hijabs aren't allowed here.

Go home and straighten your hair!

You can't come in unless you take it off!

CONSEQUENCE 4:
THERE'S A HUGE
OBSESSION WITH

YOUTH

For a woman to be considered pretty, she has to more or less look like a teenager... even if she's 60!

Amazing anti-wrinkle cream for teens!

SERIOUSLY?!

EXCEPT GUYS ARE SEEN AS
SEXIER AS THEY GET OLDER

Ew! It's almost like they want to convince girls to date older men!

PEOPLE HAVE STUDIED LOVE STORIES ON SCREEN
AND FOUND THAT EVEN THOUGH THE MEN AGE,
THEIR LOVERS ALWAYS STAY YOUNG...

1990

actor A,
age 32

actor B,
age 25

2000

actor A,
age 42

actor C,
age 29

2018

actor A,
age 60

actor D,
age 39

Not only is that a weird message to be sending, but the women have less and less work as they get older!

Um well, they could always play moms?

NOT EVEN!! MOST OFTEN THE
WOMEN WHO PLAY MOTHERS
ARE ONLY A FEW YEARS OLDER
THAN THEIR "CHILDREN"...

actor B,
age 35

actor E,
age 24

Ridiculous!!

CONSEQUENCE 5: TO TOP IT ALL OFF, WOMEN ARE ALSO ALWAYS <u>SEXUALIZED</u>!

THAT MEANS WOMEN
ARE ALWAYS SUPPOSED
TO BE <u>SEXY</u>

→   at home   at work   at war

hubba
hubba

EVEN WHEN THERE'S <u>NO REASON</u> FOR IT!!!

Even kids are
encouraged to be
sexy!!! Awful!

Just take a look at
style for children's
characters...

Or the clothes
marketed to kids

Strawberry Shortcake's new
look, for instance.

age 4
age 6
age 8
age 7
age 10

It's dangerous!!

Kids shouldn't
be sexy!

AND GROWN WOMEN
DON'T NEED TO
BE EITHER!!!

I have better
things to do!!!

Can we get five
minutes' rest over
here??

We have a right not to
care about being pretty!

AND SOME GUYS EVEN HAVE THE NERVE TO COMPLAIN!

Yeah, but it's not like _every_ guy we see on TV has muscles like Superman!

Sure, you girls have to live up to Barbie. But we've got Superman! That's tough too!

And yeah, this unrealistic image is hard for boys too, but like...

SUPERMAN and company:

muscular →

strong →

courageous →

↗ he's a hero

he saves people ←

← he represents "good"

BARBIE and company:

pretty ↘

↙ unnatural proportions

← thin

made to be looked at ↗

↖ basically only cares about fashion, love...

WE HAVE TO BE CAREFUL ABOUT WHAT THAT SYMBOLIZES!

THE GOAL OF ALL THIS IS TO KEEP GIRLS FROM BEING TOO AMBITIOUS.

Just remember the most important thing: be PRETTY.

That's it!

Be PRETTY.

THE RESULT: We never feel like we're good enough.

I made the honor roll this year...

I play clarinet super well...

but I don't look like a top model...my life's a total waste...

HOW CAN WE FIGHT ALL THAT?

1. SEE BEAUTY IN ALL BODY TYPES...

Sure, this girl is pretty...

But so are these girls!

etc. !

2. ...ABOVE ALL: BEAUTY ISN'T THAT IMPORTANT!

It's normal to want to feel pretty, and it's cool that some girls like make-up and fashion and all that! Great!

BUT IT'S NOT THE ONLY THING THAT DETERMINES OUR WORTH!!!

There's also our intelligence

our sense of humor

emotions

imagination!

interests

Kindness

etc.!!!

And above all—ABOVE ALL—beauty is never worth ruining your physical or mental health for...

SO: EAT WHEN YOU'RE HUNGRY! + DRESS HOW YOU WANT! + DO WHAT MAKES YOU HAPPY!

3. AND BOYS: USE YOUR BRAINS!!!

Do you think you're being clever when you tell a girl she's ugly?

grrr

One cool thing to do would be to talk less about women's appearances in general!

You're really funny!!!

AND GIRLS: if someone makes fun of how you look...

FART IN THEIR FACE!

36

PRIVILEGE

IN A SYSTEM OF OPPRESSION, THERE ARE TWO GROUPS OF PEOPLE:

those who benefit from it

those who suffer under it

The people who benefit have PRIVILEGE.

WHAT DOES THAT MEAN?

HAVING PRIVILEGE MEANS YOU GET BENEFITS FROM CERTAIN SOCIAL CHARACTERISTICS

When I look for a job or a place to live, for example, people never judge me based on the fact that I'm a man or that I'm white!

They judge me on my skills, my resume, etc. Things are easier for me!

WE CAN BE PRIVILEGED IN SOME WAYS BUT NOT IN OTHERS!

For example, I have privilege because I'm white, but as a woman, I'm sometimes discriminated against.

Yeah but it's not my fault I'm privileged! It's because of the systems in place.

It's true, we don't choose to be privileged or not. Society does!

PRIVILEGE IS UNFAIR: that's why it's important to recognize it and, if you have it, not to pretend you don't!

But that doesn't change the fact that you benefit from it!

INCLUSIVE LANGUAGE

IN SOME LANGUAGES, WORDS HAVE GENDER.

For instance, in French, "woman" is feminine & "stool" is masculine.

And it's not only gendered, it's sexist too!

"Le masculin l'emporte sur le féminin." *

IF YOU'RE TALKING ABOUT 100 WOMEN AND 1 (one) MAN (or 1 stool)

YOU <u>HAVE TO</u> USE A MASCULINE PRONOUN!!!

* "the masculine takes pre- cedence over the feminine." → SEXIST + <u>GROSS</u>

IT'S BECAUSE OF AN ABSURD RULE DECIDED IN THE 17th CENTURY BY A BUNCH OF DUDES.

Women are just less intelligent and important than men!

That's why!

IN ENGLISH, LUCKILY, WE HAVE A LOT OF

GENDER NEUTRAL OPTIONS!

We can say "HUMANKIND"

← instead of "MANKIND"

or

"SERVER"

instead of "WAITER/WAITRESS"

⚠ BUT THAT DOESN'T MEAN THAT SEXISM CAN'T HIDE IN LESS OBVIOUS PLACES! ⚠

When you say "nurse," do you think about a man or a woman?

And when you say "doctor," why do you think about a man?

It's very important to be aware of these things!

They're like little language traps we don't think about.

<u>IN CONCLUSION,</u> always ask yourself about the kind of assumptions you're making when you're speaking!

Gender

Gender isn't just woven into our language, it's everywhere in our society, beginning at birth when babies are assigned a gender that comes with its own set of social roles.

GIRLS =

love

beauty

mother

princess

jealousy

shoes

ETC.

BOYS =

courage

toughness

friends

Maths

√4+3
2×b =
2abc

firefighter

cool

ETC.

IT'S FRUSTRATING BECAUSE WHEN YOU HEAR OVER AND OVER THAT BOYS ARE LIKE THIS AND GIRLS ARE LIKE THAT, WE START THINKING WE'RE BORN THAT WAY!

Except...it's clear that's complete nonsense.

A newborn baby doesn't love make-up just because she's a girl!

But um...why do we assign different roles to girls and boys?

Excellent question!

BASICALLY, YOU ARE BORN AND THEN SOCIETY SAYS:

1. You have a penis = BOY = your life will be this way

2. You have a vagina = GIRL = your life will be that way

Um? HOW DOES THAT MAKE SENSE??!!

What do your genitals have to do with what you like, who you are, etc?

THERE HAVE BEEN SEVERAL STUDIES IN THE PAST FEW YEARS ON GIRLS' AND BOYS' BRAINS TO SEE IF THERE REALLY ARE DIFFERENCES.

This research wasn't even done properly! Grr!! You've got to be kidding me!

A scientist named Catherine Vidal...

studied scans of lots of different brains:

Kinda look like nuts...

WHAT SHE FOUND:

Actually, there's not much difference...

There are tiny things, like neurons to set off periods for people who have a uterus...but nothing to do with personality!

AND WHAT'S MORE, WHEN WE'RE BORN, THE BRAIN IS ONLY 10% "FINISHED"!!

↳ IT'S SHAPED THROUGH OUR ENTIRE LIVES!!

by education

school

E T C.

media

and relationships

So it's not actually about biology at all? How can something be natural if it changes throughout your entire lifetime?

Exactly!

So gender categories aren't a real thing?

Nope! Well, they're the boxes society puts us in.

BASICALLY, WE'RE TOLD THAT WE'RE BORN A CERTAIN WAY AND THAT'S THAT, SO WE DON'T STEP OUT OF OUR GENDER BOXES.

But why?

Because there's a group that benefits from it. And in this case, it's men.

41

But umm...not all the time... for example, it's frustrating that I can't cry without people making fun of me...

I don't like pretending I'm tough.

Ohh!!! Of course, I'm not saying that men are happy with their roles all the time either!

SOMETIMES IT'S HARD TO BE A GUY:

Don't cry!
Buck up!
Be strong!
Watch sports!
No pink!
Be tough!
Be brave!
Like fighting!

EXCEPT

- When a guy fulfills a certain number of "requirements" for his gender...

he gets a pile of ADVANTAGES!

No need to fulfill 'em all. Just the minimum and bingo!

 doesn't cry
 acts manly

 heyyy
seduces women

 likes "guy" stuff

 → GOOD JOBS → RESPECT E T C.

 → ADMIRED FOR THE SLIGHTEST THING

 Sure it's dumb and restrictive, but there's a reward at the end.

- But a girl can tick all the boxes...

and she'll still experience sexism and won't really get any advantages.

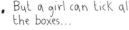

 wears make-up (but not too much)
 is sexy (but not too sexy)

 is sweet, a good listener
 is serious (but not too serious)

 → ABUSE
 → LOWER SALARY

 → HOUSEWORK
 ew → COMMENTS ABOUT HER LOOKS

E T C.

➡ AND THAT'S WHAT'S UNFAIR!

But if these roles aren't natural, does that mean we don't have to stick to them?

Exactly!

Any construction can be taken apart! We don't need to fit into weird boxes!

·GAME·

Connect the happy vulva to what it likes and the grumpy vulva to what it doesn't like.

Good grief! Your genitals don't determine what you like!

We're not playing some kind of weird matching game...

These gender boxes are stupid for plenty of different reasons.

FIRST, BIOLOGICALLY, THERE AREN'T JUST TWO OPTIONS.

Yeah that's not going to cut it, since there are dozens of other possibilities.

THERE ARE INTERSEX PEOPLE WHO DON'T FIT INTO THE TYPICAL CATEGORY OF "MALE" OR "FEMALE."

Hi!

BEING INTERSEX IS ABOUT BIOLOGICAL SEX CHARACTERISTICS, LIKE GENITALS OR HORMONES.

You can't tell just by looking at me!

SOMETIMES BEING INTERSEX IS SOMETHING KNOWN AT BIRTH, OTHER TIMES IT'S REALIZED AT PUBERTY.

⚠ CAREFUL! ⚠

Intersex people are not half-man, half-woman!

NOPE! NO NO NO

⚠ CAREFUL 2! ⚠

Being intersex has nothing to do with gender identity! Those are two different things!

You can be a girl

and intersex!

A boy

and intersex

Non-binary and intersex!

44

WHEN WE'RE BORN, SOCIETY CHOOSES A BOX (BOY OR GIRL) FOR US, AND EVEN IF IT MAKES US UNCOMFORTABLE BECAUSE IT'S A BAD SYSTEM, MOST OF THE TIME WE DEAL WITH IT AND DON'T FEEL THE NEED TO CHANGE THE BOX WE'RE IN.

BUT SOMETIMES, IT'S UNBEARABLE, AND IT FEELS LIKE WE'VE BEEN PUT IN THE WRONG BOX. AND WE REALIZE WE NEED TO CHANGE IT.

WHEN WE AREN'T PUT IN THE RIGHT BOX AT BIRTH, WE'RE <u>TRANS!</u>

People who stay in their assigned gender categories are called cisgender or cis!

We refer to someone as being transgender.

And everyone has their own trans identity!

CAREFUL! Transgender isn't a gender!!!

There's also people who don't see themselves in society's gender boxes.

Other trans identities include folks who are nonbinary and agender! Sometimes we prefer to use they/them as pronouns, instead of he/his or she/her.

You can be a trans woman.

Or a trans man!

Everyone is different! The important thing is to respect the pronouns people choose for themselves.

CAREFUL 2! A trans woman isn't a "fake woman" nor is a trans man a "fake man"!!!

CAREFUL 3! Sexual orientation (being gay, bi, or heterosexual) has nothing to do with gender identity! These are two different things!

I'm not "a woman in a man's body..."

or "a woman who was a man before."

I'm just: a woman.

GENDER IDENTITY
=
who we are!

SEXUAL ORIENTATION
=
who we like!

iN SUMMARY:

1. THERE'S A GIRL/BOY SYSTEM IMPOSED ON US, AND IT'S DUMB.
IT'S NOT BASED ON BIOLOGY OR LOGIC.

It's a system that pre-defines what people should like and how people should act based on their gender assigned at birth.

And that also helps justify one group (men) dominating another group (women)!!

The goal is to smash this system to pieces!!!

2. BUT WE STILL HAVE TO EXIST WITHIN IT, SO WE NEED TO FIND WAYS
TO MAKE IT EASIER TO DO THAT.

That can mean questioning your gender.

ugh

Or fighting for feminism!

STOP SEXUAL HARASSMENT

EQUAL PAY FOR EQUAL WORK!!

Or by refusing the gender you were assigned when it doesn't fit!

Or by doing all of this, and other stuff too!

3. THE IMPORTANT THING IS TO QUESTION THE SYSTEM AND THESE GENDER
BOXES, TO KNOW WHERE WE FIT INTO IT ALL, HOW WE'RE PRIVILEGED OR UN-
JUSTLY TREATED, AND HOW OTHERS ARE PRIVILEGED OR UNJUSTLY TREATED.

So that we don't push people down who are less privileged!

And so we can recognize injustice, and speak up and fight against it!

Yep! And most of all: RESPECT others, their identity, and their differences!

DO FEMINISTS HATE MEN ???

FEMINISM IS THE FIGHT TO END SEXISM. SO, THIS INEVITABLY MEANS THE END OF MALE PRIVILEGE!

 Huh?

 What??

 I don't see why.

 That's ridiculous!!!

 Euh... really?

A LOT OF PEOPLE (MOSTLY MEN) AREN'T SUPER STOKED ABOUT THIS...

Equality = fine, as long as nothing changes for me!

So they try to make feminism seem ridiculous by saying all sorts of things that aren't true!

Anyways feminists are just man-haters!!

They have no sense of humor!

They want us to diiiieee!

It Kinda seems like they're the ones who hate women...

All we want is real equality and an end to sexism!

Intersectionality

We've talked a lot about gender, girls, boys, and sexism....

But, as you might already know, there are lots of other Kinds of inequality.

UNFORTUNATELY, OUR SOCIETY IS BASED ON GROUPS OF PEOPLE CRUSHING OTHER GROUPS OF PEOPLE.

When it's men crushing women, it's called SEXISM, but that's not the only form of oppression that exists...

RACISM=
White people have privileges and people of color suffer because of it.

CAPITALISM =
Rich people have privileges and poor people suffer because of it.

HOMOPHOBIA =
Heterosexual people have privileges and homosexual and bisexual people suffer because of it.

TRANSPHOBIA =
Cis people have privileges and trans people suffer because of it.

ABLEISM =
Able-bodied people have privileges and people with disabilities suffer because of it.

FATPHOBIA =
Thin people have privileges and fat people suffer because of it.

(just a few examples...)

EVERY SYSTEM WORKS PRETTY MUCH THE SAME:

The people on top tell us they have a right to be there and try to convince everyone that the system works fine and can't change.

But that's simply not true!

It's ALWAYS been this way.

It's just the way it is!

It's biology, it's natural!

It makes sense!

BUT IN TRUTH, THESE SYSTEMS OF DOMINATION AREN'T NATURAL: THEY'VE BEEN CONSTRUCTED FOR CENTURIES SO THAT THE PEOPLE ON TOP CAN CONTINUE TO DOMINATE THE PEOPLE ON THE BOTTOM. IN OTHER WORDS, SO THEY CAN KEEP THEIR PRIVILEGE!

Using racist theories that said people who weren't white were inferior, white people justified slavery and exploiting people in colonized areas like Africa, for instance.

These theories are wrong and have been disproven: there's only one human race. But today, white people still have the most advantages and privileges!

I never get turned down for a job or apartment because of my skin color!

I do though...

AND GUESS WHAT? DIFFERENT FORMS OF OPPRESSION DON'T JUST PILE ON TOP OF EACH OTHER, THEY COMBINE TO CREATE NEW KINDS OF INJUSTICE.

Which means that a black woman won't experience...

the same racism as a black man

+

the same sexism as a white woman

→ SHE EXPERIENCES A FORM OF RACISM COMBINED WITH SEXISM, AND VICE VERSA

You going to blush for me, my beautiful lioness?

To speak about this, we invented a word (that's kinda tricky): INTERSECTIONALITY*

What does it mean, exactly?

*actually, a professor named Kimberlé Crenshaw came up with it!

IT MEANS THAT THESE FORMS OF OPPRESSION ADD UP AND MIX TOGETHER TO FORM A WHOLE NEW KIND OF OPPRESSION.

SEXISM

SEXISM & RACISM

RACISM HOMOPHO-BIA

RACISM HOMOPHOBIA SEXISM

HOMOPHOBIA

↳ IT'S AS IF THE PEOPLE EXPERIENCING THE INJUSTICE HAD TO RUN WHILE WEARING A BACKPACK THAT SLOWED THEM DOWN, AND THE SHAPE AND WEIGHT OF THE BAG WAS DIFFERENT DEPENDING ON THE PERSON.

WHEN WE'RE AT A DISADVANTAGE IN ONE SYSTEM, IT AFFECTS OTHER PARTS OF OUR LIVES TOO.

→ For example, it happens often that people are refused a job because of racism and sexism.

→ But it also affects the amount of money we have: there's a higher risk of being poor when it's hard to get a job!

Ah, your name is Faïza? Ah...sorry, the position is actually filled...

We were thinking more of a man. It's quite a difficult job...

+

So yeah. Life is a whole lot easier when you're a straight, white, rich guy who's in good health, etc.

Which is why when a guy like this says something like:

Well if I can make it, anyone can.

AND IT'S UNFAIR!

THAT'S A LOAD OF CRAP!!

Hey you guys, why so slow?

This is so easy!!

THE CONCEPT OF INTERSECTIONALITY HELPS US SEE HOW DIFFERENT KINDS OF INEQUALITY COMPOUND TO MAKE NEW FORMS OF INJUSTICE, AND AVOIDS SAYING ONE KIND IS WORSE THAN ANOTHER.

Because, obviously, the more privilege you have, the louder your voice is and the more people will listen to you.

So it's easy for the most privileged people to say their problems are the most urgent, most important, just because their voices are loudest!

Feminism is a rich people's fight!

Uh

but

It's important that everyone's voice is heard!

We need to listen to each other!

2. IT ALSO HELPS EXPLAIN WHY PEOPLE AFFECTED BY THE SAME PROBLEMS NEED TO SPEAK WITH ONE ANOTHER ABOUT THEM, AWAY FROM PEOPLE WHO HAVEN'T HAD THE SAME EXPERIENCE.

It's important to have safe spaces where we can concentrate on our specific problems!

3. IT HELPS US BUILD REAL ALLIANCES BETWEEN PEOPLE WHO SUFFER UNDER DIFFERENT SYSTEMS OF OP- PRESSION SO WE CAN FIGHT AGAINST THESE SYSTEMS TOGETHER!!!

INTERSECTIONALITY IS AN IMPORTANT PART OF FEMINIST MOVEMENTS BECAUSE IT GIVES <u>ALL</u> WOMEN A PLACE AND A VOICE AND FIGHTS FOR THE RIGHTS OF ALL, <u>WITHOUT EXCLUDING ANYONE</u>! THAT'S SUPER IMPORTANT!

It's important to realize some women have privi- leges that other women don't!

The fight for feminism can't just be about women who are white AND rich AND straight, etc.

We need to listen, support, and help one another!

Mirion Malle is a French cartoonist and illustrator who lives in Montreal. She studied comics at the École Superieure des Arts Saint-Luc in Brussels before pursuing a Masters degree in Sociology specializing in Gender and Feminist studies, via Paris Diderot and the Université du Québec à Montréal. Malle has published three books. *The League of Super Feminists* is her first book to be translated into English. The French edition was nominated for the 2020 Prix Jeunesse at the Angoulême International Comics Festival.